EVERYTHING I REALLY NEED TO KNOW
I LEARNED FROM TELEVISION

EVERYTHING I REALLY NEED TO KNOW
I LEARNED FROM TELEVISION

written by BARRY DUTTER

illustrated by RICK PARKER

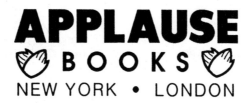

APPLAUSE
B O O K S
NEW YORK • LONDON

AN APPLAUSE ORIGINAL

EVERYTHING I REALLY NEED TO KNOW I LEARNED FROM TELEVISION
Written by Barry Dutter • Illustrated by Rick Parker
Copyright © 1993 by Barry Dutter and Rick Parker
All Rights Reserved

Library of Congress Cataloging-in-Publication Data

Dutter, Barry
    Everything I really need to know I learned from television /
written by Barry Dutter ; illustrated by Rick Parker.
      p.   cm.
   "An Applause original."
   ISBN 1-55783-122-X : $7.95
   1. Parker, Rick--Themes, motives. 2. Television--Caricatures and
cartoons. 3. American wit and humor, Pictorial. I. Parker, Rick.
II. Title.
NC1429.P268A4   1992
741.5'973--dc20

        92-27221
        CIP

APPLAUSE BOOKS
211 West 71st Street
New York, NY 10023
Phone: 212-595-4735   Fax: 212-721-2856

APPLAUSE BOOKS
406 Vale Road
Tonbridge, KENT TN9 1XR
Phone: 0732 357755   Fax: 0732 770219

FIRST APPLAUSE PRINTING: 1993

I'd like to dedicate this book to all the people who were most important to me when I was growing up: to Richie and Potsie. . .Joanie and Chachi. . .Jack and Chrissy. . .Tattoo and Mr. Roarke. . .Gopher and Isaac. . .Raj, Da-Wayne, and Rerun. . .Lucy and Desi. . .Alice and Sam the Butcher. . .Lenny and Squiggy. . .Mork and Mindy. . .Bo, Luke, and Daisy Duke. . .Fred and Barney . . .Brian and Shannon. . .Susan and Angus. . .Michelle, & Allison. . .the Fellas — Tommy, Bruce and Bill. . .Warren, John, and the two Daves. . .Leslie and Allyssa. . .to all my cousins, especially Anna, who made me write this part. . .to Mike Rockwitz, who put up with quite a lot of my and Rick's shenanigans. . .to Tom DeFalco and Mark Gruenwald of Marvel Comics for all their support. . .but most of all, I'd like to dedicate this book to my parents, RoseMarie and Ray, who let me watch as much TV as I wanted when I was a kid!

— *Barry Dutter*

The artist wishes to acknowledge all the love and support, as well as the numerous brilliant suggestions of his wife over the many months it took to do these drawings. "Lisa, I could have done it without you, but it wouldn't have been nearly as much fun."

— *Rick Parker*

The creators wish to acknowledge the following people who helped in the production of this book:

Dan Carr, Rob Carosella, Mark Bienstock, Glenn Greenberg, Mike Rockwitz, Josh Myers, John Byrne, Mike Carlin, Jim Salicrup, Jesus Gonzalez, Lisa Trusiani, "Professor" James Felder, Stu Schwartzberg, Sarra Mossoff, Mary Egrie, Glenn Herdling, Kaye Radtke and Homunculus.

IF YOU'RE A **PRIVATE EYE** AND YOU FALL IN LOVE WHILE LOOKING FOR A **KILLER**, THE PERSON YOU FALL IN LOVE WITH WILL TURN OUT TO BE THE **KILLER**.

IT IS POSSIBLE TO DRINK IN A BAR **ALL NIGHT** AND NEVER SHOW ANY SIGNS OF INTOXICATION.

IT'S INEVITABLE--
ONE DAY,
A **PRINCE** OR
PRINCESS WHO
LOOKS JUST LIKE
YOU WILL ASK
YOU TO **TRADE**
PLACES WITH
THEM.

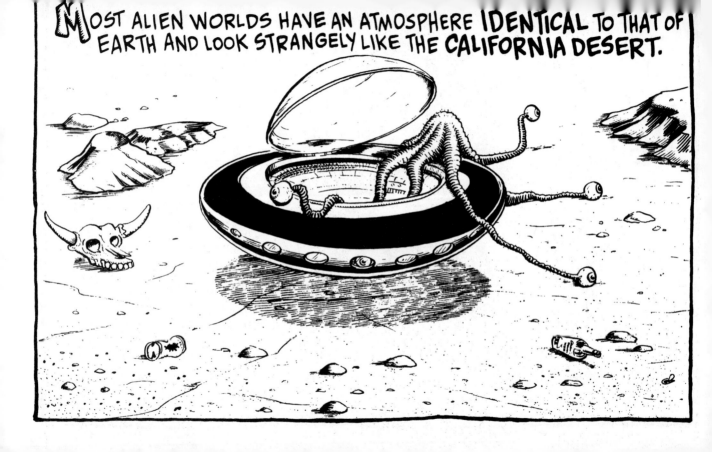

MOST PSYCHIATRISTS ARE ACTUALLY **SERIAL KILLERS**, BUT YOU'D NEVER SUSPECT THEM, BECAUSE THEY ACT SO **CALM** AND RATIONAL.

THE MORE SOMEONE REFUSES TO DO SOMETHING, THE GREATER THE PROBABILITY THEY WILL WIND UP DOING IT ANYWAY. (**EXAMPLE:** "I AM NOT TAKING OUT FAT ALICE! I AM **NOT** TAKING OUT **FAT ALICE!**"

BOING!

" I'M TAKING OUT FAT ALICE!"

ALL GUYS CARRY AROUND A **LITTLE BLACK BOOK** FULL OF GIRLS' PHONE NUMBERS.

THE PHONE NUMBERS ALL HAVE LITTLE **STARS** NEXT TO THEM EVALUATING EACH GIRL'S SEXUAL PROWESS.

YOU CAN CALL A DIFFERENT GIRL EVERY NIGHT, AND THEY'LL **ALWAYS** BE AVAILABLE WHENEVER YOU WANT TO SEE THEM.

AT SOME POINT IN YOUR LIFE, YOUR DOCTOR WILL MIX UP YOUR DIAGNOSIS AND TELL YOU THAT YOU ARE GOING TO DIE. THEN YOU WILL ACT REAL **CRAZY** FOR A COUPLE OF DAYS UNTIL YOUR DOCTOR INFORMS YOU OF HIS **MISTAKE**.

THE HIGH POINT OF ANY COURTROOM TRIAL IS THE ANNOUNCEMENT OF THE SURPRISE WITNESS.

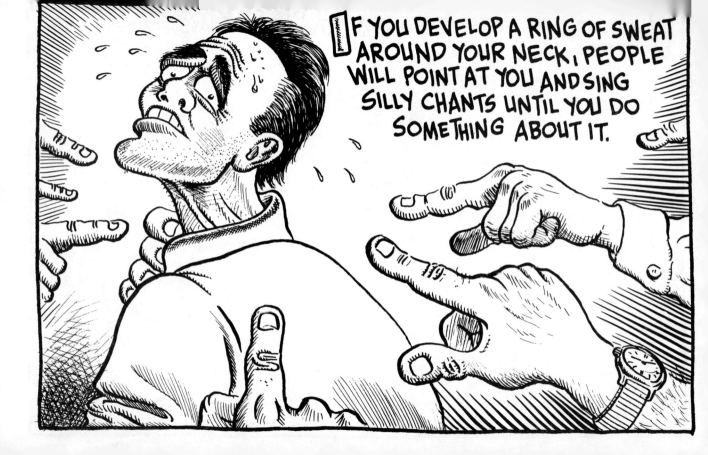

Someday you will find **FAME**, but it will not turn out to be what you **EXPECTED**.

THE NERD **ALWAYS** GETS THE HOT BABE.

IF YOU'RE A COP, YOUR PRECINCT CAPTAIN WILL YELL AT YOU A LOT, BUT **DEEP DOWN** HE REALLY **RESPECTS** YOU.

ANYONE CAN LAND A PLANE OR DELIVER A BABY. THESE ARE TWO OF THE EASIEST THINGS TO DO IN THE WORLD. IN FACT, IT'S POSSIBLE TO DO **BOTH** AT ONCE.

ANY TIME A MAN GETS IN A COMPETITION WITH A WOMAN, THE WOMAN WILL ALWAYS WIN.